100 FROZEN YOGURT RECIPES

HOMEMADE EASY AND DELICIOUS SUMMER DESSERTS

JUSTIN RAMSEY

INTRODUCTION

People have been enjoying frozen yogurt for over four decades. The popular snack originated in India and gradually gained popularity in the United States. As a lower fat alternative to soft serve ice cream, frozen yogurt quickly became widespread and available in many forms. Certain brands of the dessert also contain beneficial bacterial cultures and strains. This further fueled public demand and provided consumers with good cause to eat up.

Many retailers now allow for the customization of frozen yogurt with the addition of toppings and fruits. The recipes in this book are based upon the popular flavors that are selling in store, as well as unique recipes which have worked well when entertaining. Please note that some of the recipes require the use of an ice cream maker for ease of cooking.

You will quickly find that making your own yogurt is quite easy, and in many cases it is much tastier and fresher coming from your own kitchen. Fewer binding agents and preservatives are needed in this case. It is also a fun way to get the kids involved in food preparation and cooking. My family certainly enjoys an occasional frozen yogurt dessert and I hope yours will too!

Justin

TABLE OF CONTENTS

BASIC VANILLA FROZEN YOGURT

We take you back to the beginning with this yummy base recipe. This basic vanilla frozen yogurt is delicious on its own or mixed with fruit puree if you want to switch up the flavors.

Makes: 6 Serves
Prep: 10 minutes plus 4 hours freezing time

Ingredients:
2 Cups Whole Milk Yogurt
3.5oz Unrefined Caster Sugar
3.5oz White Sugar
1 Tsp Vanilla Extract
1/4 Tsp Salt

Directions
1. In a bowl whisk together the yogurt, sugars, and salt until they are well incorporated and dissolved
2. Put the mix into a plastic container and freeze for one hour. Take out and beat with a whisk to break up the ice crystals
3. Freeze again for another hour
4. Whisk again and refreeze for another hour
5. Whisk again and freeze for one hour undisturbed before serving

BLOOD ORANGE FROZEN YOGURT CREAMSICLES

Enjoy this tart take on old school creamsicles with more sophisticated blood orange popsicles. Sweeter than normal oranges and with a pretty pink hue, these popsicles may remind you of your childhood but they are also a very grown up affair.

Makes: 8 Serves
Prep: 10 minutes plus 3 hours freezing time

Ingredients:
2 Cups Blood Orange Juice
2 Cups Greek Yogurt
1 Tbsp Blood Orange Zest
1/3 Cup Date Syrup
1 Tsp Vanilla Essence

Directions
1. In a bowl whisk together the blood orange juice and yogurt until well mixed and smooth and creamy in consistency
2. Add the date syrup and vanilla essence and mix thoroughly until well combined
3. Pour into popsicle molds and freeze for at least 3 hours

STRAWBERRY SHORTCAKE FROZEN YOGURT

Harness the delicious flavors of classic strawberry shortcake with this frozen yogurt version that is easy to make and simply divine.

Makes: 8 Serves
Prep: 20 minutes plus 4 hours freezing time

Ingredients:
1 Punnet Strawberries, hulled
2 Cups Greek Yogurt
1 Can Condensed Milk
1 Tsp Vanilla Bean Paste
1 Cup Double Cream
8 Pieces Shortbread, crushed with a rolling pin

Directions
1. First, make a puree with the strawberries by placing them in a blender and blending to a smooth paste. Keep a handful of strawberries aside for garnish
2. Add the Greek yogurt, the condensed milk and the vanilla paste to the blender and pulse to combine thoroughly
3. Whip the cream in a bowl until soft peaks form
4. Add 1/3 of the strawberry puree and mix. Repeat until all the puree is incorporated
5. Pour 1/4 of the mixture into a plastic container then sprinkle over 1/4 of the shortbread pieces and extra strawberries. Then cover with another layer of mixture. Repeat until all the ingredients are used up. Make sure the top layer is made up of biscuits and strawberries
6. Freeze for 4 hours before serving

BANANA CHIP FROZEN YOGURT

Like the banana ice cream you used to enjoy as a child but lighter, fresher, and with the addition of crunchy banana chips to add texture.

Makes: 6 Serves
Prep: 20 minutes plus 4 hours freezing time

Ingredients:
4 Ripe Bananas, peeled
2 Cups Greek Yogurt
1 Cup Condensed Milk
A Large Handful of Banana Chips (avoid if they are heavily salted)

Directions
1. Puree the bananas, yogurt and milk in a blender until silky in consistency and pour into a plastic container
2. Place the banana chips in a bag and bash with a rolling pin to make banana crumbs
3. Sprinkle the crumbs on top of the yogurt mixture and then make swirling patterns using a knife so that the crumbs are marbled throughout
4. Cover and freeze for at least 4 hours

RUM AND RAISIN FROZEN YOGURT

Rum and raisin is a classic combination for a reason. It's simply delicious! This recipe takes time to allow the flavors to develop but is well worth it and soaking the raisins with the yogurt ensures that you get a plump and juicy result even after several hours in the freezer.

Makes: 8 Serves
Prep: 20 minutes plus 8 hours + 4 hours freezing time

Ingredients:
3 Cups Coconut Yogurt
2/3 Cup Sugar
2/3 Cup Raisins
2 Tbsps Dark Rum
2 Tsps Vanilla Extract
A Pinch of Salt

Directions
1. Put the coconut yogurt in a strainer lined with cheesecloth and place over a pot. Leave in the fridge for at least 8 hours until all the water has drained out of the yoghurt
2. Mix the strained yogurt with the sugar, raisins, rum, vanilla, and salt until well combined
3. Cover and place in the fridge overnight to allow the flavors to develop
4. Place the mixture in an ice cream maker and follow the instructions for frozen yogurt and then freeze for 4 hours

CHAI TEA FROZEN YOGURT

This lightly spiced and aromatic combination is a nod to the chai tea latte but this time in frozen yogurt form. It's easy to make with an ice cream maker and evokes all the flavors of Indian sweet tea.

Makes: 4 Serves
Prep: 15 minutes plus 4 hours freezing time

Ingredients:
2 Chai Teabags
3/4 Cups Water
32oz Vanilla Greek Yogurt
Pinch of Cinnamon
Pinch of Cardamom
Pinch of Ground Ginger
1 Tbsp Sugar

Directions
1. Steep the chai teabags in boiling water and then leave to cool completely
2. Mix all the ingredients in a bowl and add the cooled tea
3. Place in an ice cream maker and follow the instructions for frozen yogurt
4. Put in the freezer for 4 hours or eat immediately if you prefer a softer consistency

INSTANT VERY BERRY FROZEN YOGURT

This clever little recipe allows you to skip the freezing stage all together and makes instant frozen yogurt that is bursting with the flavor of berries that you can eat immediately!

Makes: 4 Serves
Prep: 15 minutes

Ingredients:
8oz Frozen Mixed Berries
8oz Greek Yogurt
1 Tbsp Honey

Directions
1. Place the frozen berries, yogurt and honey in a blender and blitz for 20 seconds. The mixture should come together in a ball and have the consistency of ice cream
2. Serve immediately

BLACKBERRY AND LAVENDER FROZEN YOGURT POPSICLES

These gorgeous frozen yogurt popsicles are a lovely shade of purple and are perfumed with the delicate fragrance of lavender throughout, mixed with the sharpness of summer blackberries.

Makes: 6 Serves
Prep: 20 minutes plus 5 hours freezing time

Ingredients:
13oz Greek Yogurt
3/4 Cup Milk
4 Tbsps Blackberry Jam
2 Punnets Fresh Blackberries
1 Tbsp Vanilla Extract
1 Tsp Dried Lavender

Directions
1. Put the yogurt, milk, jam, blackberries, and vanilla in a blender and blitz until smooth. Add the lavender and pulse to combine
2. Pour into molds and freeze for 5 hours before serving

CHEESECAKE FROZEN YOGURT POPS

These frozen yogurt popsicles are like a pop of frozen blueberry cheesecake on a stick. There is no baking required and they use the best of summer blueberries that add a lovely lavender tone.

Makes: 6 Serves
Prep: 25 minutes plus 4 hours freezing time

Ingredients:
1 Packet Graham Crackers
8oz Can Condensed Milk
18oz Blueberries (about two punnets)
1 Cup Greek Yogurt

Directions
1. Put the graham crackers in a food processor and pulse until they resemble breadcrumbs
2. Add 2 tablespoons of the condensed milk and blitz again until the crumbs come together and begin to form a ball
3. Divide between 8 paper cups and press down firmly so that the crumbs hold their shape
4. Place half the blueberries, condensed milk, and yogurt in a blender and blend until smooth and silky in consistency
5. Add the remaining blueberries and pulse briefly to roughly chop
6. Pour into the paper cups on top of the breadcrumbs
7. Place a layer of cling film over each cup and then insert a wooden popsicle stick in each one. The cling film will help to hold the stick in place
8. Freeze for 4 hours and then serve

MATCHA GREEN TEA FROZEN YOGURT WITH SESAME SEEDS

Harness the detoxifying powers of green tea with this delicious Asian inspired recipe that uses matcha green tea powder to create a subtle smoky taste and light green hue. Toasted sesame seeds added at the end give crunch and color.

Makes: 6 Serves
Prep: 10 minutes plus 4 hours freezing time

Ingredients:
2 Cups Greek Yogurt
7oz Caster Sugar
2 Tbsps Matcha Green Tea Powder
4 Tbsps Toasted Sesame Seeds

Directions
1. Whisk together the yogurt, sugar, matcha powder until the sugar dissolves
2. Pour into an ice cream machine and follow the directions for frozen yogurt
3. Pour into a freezer safe container and sprinkle the toasted sesame seeds on top
4. Freeze for 4 hours and then serve

ELDERFLOWER FROZEN YOGURT

Enjoy the floral notes of this delicious and light elderflower frozen yogurt that uses elderflower cordial to inject a burst of fruity flavor.

Makes: 6 Serves
Prep: 10 minutes plus 4 hours freezing time

Ingredients:
1 Cup Greek Yogurt
2/3 Cup Milk
7oz Sugar
3 Tbsps Elderflower Cordial

Directions
1. Whisk together the yogurt, sugar, and milk until the sugar dissolves
2. Add the elderflower cordial and mix well to combine. Taste and add more sugar or cordial as necessary
3. Pour into an ice cream machine and follow the directions for frozen yogurt
4. Freeze for 4 hours and then serve

BEETROOT AND LEMON FROZEN YOGURT

Try something different with this light and refreshing frozen yogurt recipe that uses unusual ingredients to great effect. The beetroot adds a natural earthy sweetness and the lemon cuts through with a tart accompaniment. Perfect for a summer barbecue or picnic.

Makes: 8 Serves
Prep: 20 minutes plus 2 hours chilling time and 4 hours freezing time

Ingredients
2 Tbsps Butter
1/2 Cup Heavy Cream
3/4 Cup Cane Sugar
1/4 Cup Roasted Beetroot
1/2 Cup Lemon Juice
1 Tbsp Lemon Zest
2 Cups Whole Milk Yogurt
1 Tbsp Cornstarch
3 Tbsps Cream Cheese

Directions
1. Melt the butter over a low heat and then remove and mix in the cream and sugar, stirring continuously. Return to a low heat and stir until the sugar is dissolved
2. Remove from the heat and leave to cool slightly then add the yogurt and mix to combine
3. Blend the beetroot, lemon juice, and zest in a blender until pureed
4. Add the cornstarch and cream cheese and blend again
5. Add the beetroot puree to the yogurt mixture and chill in the fridge for 2 hours
6. Place in an ice cream maker and follow the instructions.

7. Freeze for 4 hours before serving

CARDAMOM AND LIME FROZEN YOGURT

Think outside the box with this refreshing summer treat that mixes spicy and aromatic ground cardamom with punchy lime for an exciting flavor combination that will tickle your palette.

Makes: 6 Serves
Prep: 20 minutes plus 4 hours freezing time

Ingredients:
1/2 Cup Lime Juice
1 Tbsp Lime Zest
1/4oz Gelatin
2/3 Cup Sugar
2 Tsps Ground Cardamom
1/4 Corn Syrup
1 Cup Whole Milk Yogurt
1/2 Cup Heavy Cream

Directions
1. Sprinkle the gelatin powder over 2 tablespoons of lime juice in a bowl and leave for 5 minutes
2. Whisk the remaining lime juice with the sugar and corn syrup and stir over a medium heat until the sugar dissolves
3. Remove and stir in the gelatin until it is fully dissolved
4. In a separate bowl combine the yogurt, lime zest, and powdered cardamom. Add the lime juice mix and stir well
5. Add the cream and whisk to incorporate
6. Place in the fridge until cold and then transfer to an ice cream maker
7. Follow the instructions for frozen yoghurt and then freeze for 4 hours before serving

BLUEBERRY RIPPLE FROZEN YOGURT

Just like the raspberry ripple ice cream you used to enjoy as a child, this lighter version uses the humble blueberry for a fun twist.

Makes: 8 Serves
Prep: 30 minutes plus 6 hours freezing time

Ingredients:
1 ¼ Cup Full Fat Milk
Zest of 1 Orange
1 Egg
2 Egg Yolks
2oz Caster Sugar
1 Tsp Corn Flour
1 Tsp Vanilla Extract
8oz Greek Yoghurt
4oz Blueberries
1oz Caster Sugar
4oz Blueberries for decoration

Directions
1. Heat the milk and orange zest in a pan until boiling
2. In a bowl place the eggs, egg yolks, sugar, corn flour, and vanilla and whisk until fluffy
3. Add the milk to the bowl and then return to the heat and stir over a low heat until the mixture is thick and coats that back of a spoon. Remove and leave to cool
4. When cooled, add the yogurt and mix well
5. Put in an ice cream maker and follow the instructions for frozen yogurt and then place in the freezer for 2 hours
6. In the meantime, make a fruit puree using half of the blueberries

7. Cook the blueberries in a pan with the sugar and a splash of water, boil and reduce and then pulse in a blender
8. Pass through a sieve to remove any seeds
9. Take the frozen yogurt out of the freezer and beat with a balloon whisk to break up any ice crystals
10. Using a spoon, ripple the blueberry puree throughout the frozen yogurt and return to the freezer
11. Freeze for a further 4 hours and then serve

PEAR AND CINNAMON FROZEN YOGURT

Celebrate the tastes of Christmas with this classic combination of pears and cinnamon, all in frozen yogurt form!

Makes: 6 Serves
Prep: 20 minutes plus 4 hours freezing time

Ingredients:
1 Tin Pears
1 Cup Vanilla Greek Yogurt
4 Tbsps Sugar
1/2 Tsp Ground Cinnamon
1/4 Tsp Ground Allspice

Directions
1. Drain the pears and reserve half of the juice. Place the pears in a blender and puree until smooth
2. In a bowl, mix the pears, juice, yogurt, sugar, cinnamon and allspice
3. Transfer to an ice cream machine and follow the instructions for frozen yogurt
4. Freeze for 4 hours before serving

COOKIE DOUGH FROZEN YOGURT

This dessert takes a classic cookie dough ice cream recipe and switches it up by making a tarter and lighter frozen yogurt version.

Makes: 8 Serves
Prep: 20 minutes plus 4 hours freezing time

Ingredients:
1/2 Cup Butter
1/2 Cup Brown Sugar
1/4 Cup White Sugar
2 Tsps Vanilla Extract
1 Cup Flour
1/4 Tsp Baking Soda
1/4 Tsp Salt
3/4 Cup Chocolate Chips
1 Cup Vanilla Yogurt

Directions
1. Beat the butter, vanilla extract, and sugars together with a hand mixer until fluffy
2. In a separate bowl, mix the flour, baking soda, and salt
3. Add the chocolate chips and stir again
4. Add the flour mixture to the butter and fold
5. Add the yogurt and mix gently until well combined
6. Cover and freeze for 4 hours before serving

WATERMELON FROZEN YOGURT

Cool off in the warmer months with this watermelon frozen yogurt recipe, which is a play on a traditional fruit sorbet with added creaminess from the tart yogurt.

Makes: 8 Serves
Prep: 20 minutes plus 4 hours freezing time

Ingredients:
1/4 Cup Water
1/4 Cup Sugar
4 Cups Watermelon, diced and seeds removed
1 Cup Vanilla Greek Yogurt
1 Tbsp Lime Juice

Directions
1. Mix the water and sugar in a saucepan and cook over a high heat stirring continuously until the sugar dissolves
2. Leave to cool
3. Place the watermelon in a blender and blend until smooth
4. Put the watermelon in a bowl and add the sugar syrup, lime juice, and yogurt
5. Pass through a metal sieve and discard any pulp that has not been broken down
6. Put the mixture in an ice cream maker and follow the setting for frozen yogurt
7. Freeze for at least 4 hours

LEMON CURD FROZEN YOGURT

For the perfect mix of tart and sweet try this delicious frozen yogurt recipe that mixes luxurious lemon curd with creamy Greek yogurt.

Makes: 8 Serves
Prep: 5 minutes plus 3 hours freezing time

Ingredients:
4 Cups Greek Yogurt
3.5oz Lemon Curd
1 Tbsp Honey

Directions
1. Mix the ingredients together in a bowl until well combined
2. Place in an ice cream maker and follow the instructions for frozen yogurt
3. Place in the freezer for at least 3 hours before serving

CHOCOLATE AND RASPBERRY FROZEN YOGURT POPS

Mix two old favorites, chocolate and raspberry to make these cute pops that are bursting with flavor and look great for birthday parties or other events. The addition of chocolate chips and makes these a riot of flavor and texture.

Makes: 8 Serves
Prep: 15 minutes plus 6 hours freezing time

Ingredients:
2 Cups Raspberries
2 Cups Greek Yogurt
3 Tbsps Sugar
1/2 Cup Chocolate Chips

Directions
1. Place the raspberries, yogurt, and sugar in a blender and blitz until smooth
2. Transfer the mixture to a bowl and swirl in the chocolate chips
3. Pour the mixture into mold and freeze for 6 hours

CHERRY CHEESECAKE FROZEN YOGURT

With a mixture of cherries, chocolate, and graham crackers, this frozen yogurt recipe tastes exactly like a big piece of cherry cheesecake!

Makes: 8 Serves
Prep: 5 minutes plus 3 hours freezing time

Ingredients:
8oz Cream Cheese
8oz Caster Sugar
1 Tbsp Lemon Juice
20oz Greek Yogurt
10oz Cherries, pitted and quartered

Directions
1. Mix the cream cheese with the sugar and lemon juice until smooth
2. Add the yoghurt until well combined
3. Swirl in the cherries
4. Place in an ice cream maker and follow the instruction for frozen yogurt
5. Freeze for 4 hours before serving

HALLOWEEN SPICED PUMPKIN FROZEN YOGURT

Perfect for Halloween or for any time of the year when pumpkins are in abundance. This pumpkin frozen yogurt is lightly spiced with cinnamon to give the perfect hit of sweet and spicy!

Makes: 5 Serves
Prep: 10 minutes plus 2 hours freezing time

Ingredients:
2 Cups Greek Yogurt
15oz Pumpkin, steamed
1/3 Cup Honey
1 Tsp Cinnamon

Directions
1. Mix the ingredients together in a blender until the pumpkin has broken down and the mixture forms a puree
2. Freeze in an ice cream maker and follow the instructions for frozen yogurt
3. Freeze for 2 hours before serving

BANANA-COCONUT FROZEN YOGURT POPSICLES

If you want to feel like you are on a tropical vacation, then look no further than these fun popsicles that are full of summery flavors and exotic notes.

Makes: 8 Serves
Prep: 20 minutes plus 5 hours freezing time

Ingredients:
13oz Greek Yogurt
2 Bananas
1/2 Cup Milk
1/2 Cup Coconut Milk
3 Tbsps Honey
A Handful of Desiccated Coconut

Directions
1. Mix the yogurt, bananas, milk, coconut milk, and honey in a blender until smooth
2. Add the coconut and pulse to mix
3. Pour into molds and freeze for 5 hours before serving

ROSEWATER FROZEN YOGURT

A very grown up twist on frozen yogurt, enjoy the sophisticated flavors at play here with this fragrant recipe that uses lightly spiced cinnamon and aromatic rosewater.

Makes: 8 Serves
Prep: 10 minutes plus 6 hours chilling and 6 hours freezing time

Ingredients:
1 1/2 Cups Heavy Cream
1 1/8 Cups Sugar
3 Cups Greek Yogurt
2 Tsps Ground Cardamom
3 Tbsps Rosewater

Directions
1. Mix the cream and sugar in a pan over a low heat until the sugar has dissolved
2. In a separate bowl mix the yogurt, cardamom and rosewater until well combined
3. Whisk in the cream in a continuous stream until smooth
4. Chill for at least 6 hours in the fridge
5. Pour into an ice cream maker and follow the instructions for frozen yogurt
6. Freeze for 6 hours before serving

VEGAN COCONUT FROZEN YOGURT

Frozen yogurt is known for being a healthier alternative to ice cream but many recipes also use heavy cream or milk making it unsuitable for vegans. Here is a vegan frozen yogurt recipe that uses soothing coconut instead of dairy.

Makes: 8 Serves
Prep: 5 minutes plus 4 hours freezing time

Ingredients:
2 Tbsps Water
1/4 Cup Date Syrup
2 Cups Coconut Yoghurt
1/2 Tsp Vanilla Extract
1/4 Cup Unsweetened Coconut, shredded

Directions
1. Mix all of the ingredients in a bowl until thoroughly combined
2. Place in an ice cream maker and follow the instructions for frozen yogurt
3. Freeze for 4 hours and sprinkle with extra coconut for decoration before serving

MEXICAN CHOCOLATE FROZEN YOGURT

Like a glass of spicy Mexican hot chocolate, but this time in frozen form! This recipe mixes classic chocolate flavors with a hit of Mexican spice for an unexpected twist.

Makes: 8 Serves
Prep: 10 minutes plus 2 hours chilling time and 3 hours freezing time

Ingredients:
4 Cups Greek Yogurt
1/2 Cup Cocoa Powder
1/2 Cup Sugar
1/4 Cup Honey
3 Tbsps Water
1 Tsp Chili Powder
2 Tsps Cinnamon
1 Tsp Vanilla Extract
1/2 Tsp Salt

Directions
1. Over a medium heat mix the cocoa powder, sugar, honey, and water until the sugar is dissolved
2. Remove and leave to cool
3. In a separate bowl combine the yogurt, cooled sugar mixture, spices, vanilla and salt
4. Refrigerate for 2 hours then place in an ice cream maker and follow the instructions
5. Freeze for 3 hours before serving

FROZEN DAIQUIRI FROZEN YOGURT

Everyone loves a frozen daiquiri, and this time you can have it as a grown-up frozen yogurt treat instead of in a glass. It's just as easy to make and even easier to enjoy!

Makes: 10 Serves
Prep: 10 minutes plus 4 hours freezing time

Ingredients:
4 Cups Greek Yogurt
1/2 Cup Heavy Cream
2/3 Cup Sugar
1 Pint Fresh Strawberries
2 Tbsps Rum

Directions
1. Place the strawberries in a blender with the rum and sugar and blend until pureed
2. Add the yogurt and cream and blitz again to combine
3. Place in the fridge for 1 hour to cool
4. Put in an ice cream maker and follow the frozen yogurt instructions
5. Freeze for 4 hours before serving

IRISH CREAM FROZEN YOGURT

Irish cream makes a perfect frozen yogurt recipe to bring you a lightly boozy dessert that is sure to win over any guest at a dinner party.

Makes: 10 Serves
Prep: 20 minutes plus 4 hours freezing time

Ingredients:
2 Tbsps Water
1 Tsp Gelatin
3oz Chocolate, chopped
3/4 Cup Milk
1/4 Cup Honey
1/4 Cup Sugar
3 Tbsps Baileys Irish Cream
1 Cup Greek Yogurt
1 Egg White
1/2 Cup Water
2/3 Cup Milk Powder

Directions
1. Mix 2 tablespoons of water and gelatin and set aside for 1 minute. Then add to a pan and stir over a low heat until dissolved
2. In a separate saucepan mix the chocolate, milk, honey and sugar. Stir until silky then mix in the gelatin and leave to cool
3. Add the Irish Cream to the cooled chocolate followed by the yogurt. Whisk the egg white, 1/3 cup water and the milk powder to soft peaks. Gently fold into the yogurt mixture, being careful not to beat the air out of the mix
4. Freeze in an ice cream maker according to the instructions for frozen yogurt and leave for 4 hours

PEACH FROZEN YOGURT

Enjoy gorgeous summer peaches with this fruity and tangy peach frozen yogurt recipe that is a stunning shade of orange and packed full of flavor.

Makes: 4 Serves
Prep: 5 minutes plus 4 hours freezing time

Ingredients:
4 Cups Peaches, frozen
2 Tbsps Honey
1/2 Cup Yogurt
1 Tbsp Lemon Juice

Directions
1. Put the peaches, honey, yogurt and lemon juice in a blender and process until smooth
2. As the peaches are frozen you can serve this as frozen yogurt immediately or freeze and eat at another time

FRESH MINT FROZEN YOGURT

Most mint recipes don't use fresh mint but luckily this one does so you will get the freshest herbal blast in a tart and yummy yogurt.

Makes: 6 Serves
Prep: 20 minutes plus 4 hours freezing time

Ingredients:
1 Cup Fresh Mint Leaves
1 Cup Heavy Cream
1/2 Cup Honey
2 Cups Greek Yogurt
2oz Chocolate Chips

Directions
1. Tear the mint and place in a pan with the cream over a medium heat. Bring to a simmer and add the honey
2. Leave to cool
3. Sieve and discard the mint leaves
4. Add the yogurt and whisk until thoroughly combined
5. Chill for 30 minutes in the fridge
6. Place in an ice cream maker and follow the instructions
7. When the frozen yogurt is ready stir in the chocolate chips and freeze for 4 hours

VIOLET FROZEN YOGURT

A gorgeous lavender frozen yogurt that uses violet extract for a soft and delicately perfumed dessert.

Makes: 6 Serves
Prep: 10 minutes plus 3 hours freezing time

Ingredients:
1/4 Cup Sugar
1 Cup Greek Yoghurt
1 Cup Heavy Cream
1/4 Tsp Natural Violet Extract
Natural Purple Food Coloring

Directions
1. Mix the heavy cream, sugar, and violet extract in a pan over a low heat until the sugar is dissolved and then leave to cool
2. Add the yoghurt to the cooled mixture and mix well
3. Add a splash of food coloring to achieve a light lavender color and mix well
4. Freeze in an ice cream maker according to the instructions for frozen yogurt and freeze for 4 hours
5. Serve decorated with violet flowers

EGGNOG HOLIDAY FROZEN YOGURT

A festive treat for the holidays that is perfect for when you just want to splurge. This frozen yogurt is creamy, decadent, and completely moreish.

Makes: 8 Serves
Prep: 10 minutes plus 1 hour freezing time

Ingredients:
1½ Cups Greek Yogurt
1⅓ Cups Eggnog, homemade or store bought
1 Cup Sugar
1 Tsp Vanilla Essence
Pinch of Nutmeg
Pinch of Cinnamon

Directions
1. Mix all the ingredients together in a bowl until well incorporated. Place in the fridge for at least 8 hours or overnight
2. Pour into an ice cream maker and follow the instructions for frozen yogurt
3. Freeze for at least one hour before serving

MANGO TANGO FROZEN YOGURT

A cross between a traditional fruit sorbet and ice cream, this mango tango frozen yoghurt is sweet, tart, and creamy all at the same time.

Makes: 8 Serves
Prep: 10 minutes plus 4 hours freezing time

Ingredients:
6oz Mango, cut into chunks
2 Cups Greek Yogurt
2/3 Cup Honey
Juice of 1 Lime

Directions
1. Over a low heat simmer the mango, honey, and lime juice in a saucepan for 15 minutes
2. Leave to cool
3. Blend in a blender until smooth
4. In a large bowl mix the fruit puree and the yogurt until well combined
5. Refrigerate for 4 hours
6. Place in an ice cream maker and follow the manufacturer's instructions for frozen yogurt
7. Place in a freezer safe container and freeze for at least 4 hours before serving

AVOCADO FROZEN YOGURT

A slightly unusual frozen yogurt recipe, but in many Asian countries avocado is eaten as a dessert. Here it makes a deliciously creamy frozen treat for a hot day.

Makes: 8 Serves
Prep: 10 minutes plus 4 hours freezing time

Ingredients:
1 Ripe Avocado
2 Cups Greek Yogurt
1/2 Cup Full Fat Milk
1/2 Tsp Vanilla Extract
4 Tbsps Caster Sugar

Directions
1. Put the flesh of the avocado and place all other ingredients in a blender and pulse until smooth
2. Place in a freezer safe container, stir, and cover then freeze for 3 hours, taking the mixture out of the freezer and whisking every half an hour to break up any ice crystals that are forming
3. Serve garnished with additional avocado slices

WHITE CHOCOLATE FROZEN YOGURT

This recipe is a variation away from the standard cocoa based chocolate flavors. White chocolate tastes great garnished with with fruit puree if you want to switch up the flavors.

Makes: 8 Serves
Prep: 20 minutes plus 4 hours chilling time and 6 hours freezing time

Ingredients:
1 Cup Coconut Milk
3/4 Cup White Chocolate Chips
2 Cups Greek Yogurt
1/2 Cup Honey
1 Tsp Vanilla Extract
1/8 Tsp Salt

Directions
1. Place the white chocolate chips in a heatproof bowl over a pan of simmering water. Stir until the chocolate chips have melted
2. Leave to cool slightly then whisk in the coconut milk until smooth
3. In a separate bowl, whisk the yogurt, honey, vanilla and salt together until fully combined
4. Add the chocolate mixture and stir until incorporated
5. Chill in the refrigerator for 4 hours
6. Put in an ice cream maker and follow the directions for frozen yogurt
7. Freeze for 6 hours and then serve

WHITE WINE FROZEN YOGURT

A fantastic dessert to serve at a dinner party, this grown up frozen yogurt recipe is light and refreshing with a nip of white wine.

Makes: 8 Serves
Prep: 10 minutes plus 3 hours freezing time

Ingredients:
2 Cups Whole Milk Yogurt or Greek Yogurt
3/4 Cup Sugar
3/4 Cup Dry White Wine
Lemon Juice to taste

Directions
1. Whisk the yogurt and sugar together in a bowl until the sugar has dissolved
2. Stir in the wine then add a squeeze of lemon juice and a pinch of salt and taste
3. Add more lemon juice and salt as required
4. Place in an ice cream maker and follow the directions for frozen yogurt
5. Transfer to a freezer-proof container and freeze for 3 hours before serving

PEANUT BUTTER FROZEN YOGURT

Old-school peanut butter meets frozen yogurt in this easy recipe that doesn't even require an ice cream maker or any cooking.

Makes: 8 Serves
Prep: 10 minutes plus 3 hours freezing time

Ingredients:
2 Cups Vanilla Greek Yogurt
1/2 Cup Peanut Butter
1/4 Tsp Salt
1/3 Cup Sugar

Directions
1. Place all the ingredients in a blender and blitz until smooth
2. Transfer the mixture to a freezer-safe container and freeze for 3 hours, removing from the freezer and whisking every half an hour to break up any ice crystals
3. Serve as desired

PISTACHIO FROZEN YOGURT

A classic recipe that is similar to the much loved favorite pistachio ice cream, but with a lighter consistency and airy flavor.

Makes: 8 Serves
Prep: 10 minutes plus 4 hours freezing time

Ingredients:
6 Cups Greek Yogurt
1 ½ Cups Plain Milk
2 Tbsps Cornstarch
4 Tbsps Cream Cheese
1/2 Cup Heavy Cream
2/3 Cup Sugar
1/4 Cup Corn Syrup
1/2 Cup Pistachios, unsalted

Directions
1. In a frying pan over a medium heat dry fry the pistachios for about 10 minutes until toasted and starting to color
2. Remove and blend in a food processor until they form a paste
3. Mix 3 tablespoons of milk with the cornstarch to make a paste
4. Whisk the cream cheese with the pistachio paste
5. In a saucepan over a medium heat mix the remaining milk, cream, sugar, and corn syrup and bring to the boil
6. Remove from the heat and add the cornstarch paste, whisking slowly
7. Return to the heat and stir until the mixture has thickened and coats the back of a spoon then remove again
8. Whisk the milk mixture with the cream cheese and pistachio mix until well combined
9. Mix in the yogurt and stir to incorporate

10. Place in the refrigerator for 1 hour until chilled
11. Put in an ice cream maker and process according to the directions for frozen yogurt
12. Freeze for 4 hours before serving

GINGER-LEMON FROZEN YOGURT

A deeply refreshing frozen yogurt recipe that mixes the delicious herbal flavors of ginger with the zing of lemon juice and zest to create an aromatic dessert that is perfect at any time.

Makes: 10 Serves
Prep: 10 minutes plus 2 hours freezing time

Ingredients:
8 Cups Greek Yogurt
1/2 Cup Honey
3/4 Cup Sugar
3 Tbsps Lemon Juice
2 Tsps Lemon Zest
1 Tbsp Fresh Ginger, grated
1/4 Cup Crystallized Ginger

Directions
1. Mix the yogurt, honey, sugar, lemon juice, lemon zest and fresh ginger in a bowl
2. Place in an ice cream maker and follow the directions for frozen yogurt
3. Gently mix in the crystallized ginger
4. Freeze for 4 hours before serving

BIRTHDAY CAKE FROZEN YOGURT

The only recipe you need for a special celebration! This birthday cake frozen yogurt dessert is so easy it only uses 3 ingredients.

Makes: 8 Serves
Prep: 5 minutes plus 4 hours freezing time

Ingredients:
3 Cups Whole Milk Yogurt or Greek Yogurt
1/2 Cup Sugar
1/2 Cup Yellow Cake Mix

Directions
1. In a bowl mix together the yogurt, sugar, and cake mix
2. Place in an ice cream maker and follow the directions for frozen yogurt
3. Freeze for 4 hours before serving

COFFEE FROZEN YOGURT

Enjoy your morning cup of coffee in a whole new way with this sophisticated frozen yogurt recipe that harnesses the flavors of espresso.

Makes: 6 Serves
Prep: 10 minutes plus 4 hours freezing time

Ingredients:
1 Cup Espresso
1 Cup Greek Yogurt
1/2 Cup Milk
1/2 Cup Heavy Cream
2/3 Cup Sugar

Directions
1. Mix together all the ingredients in a bowl until smooth and well incorporated
2. Chill for 30 minutes in the refrigerator
3. Place in the freezer for 4 hours and then serve

HIBISCUS FROZEN YOGURT

A novel flavor profile for a frozen yogurt that makes a tart and floral dessert that is perfect for impressing guests at a party.

Makes: 10 Serves
Prep: 30 minutes plus 4 hours freezing time

Ingredients:
6 Cups Greek Yogurt
Zest and Juice of 3 Limes
2/3 plus 3 Tbsps Sugar
1 ½ Cups Whole Milk
2 Tbsps Cornstarch
2oz Cream Cheese
1/2 Cup Heavy Cream
1/4 Cup Light Corn Syrup
1 ½ Tsps Dried Hibiscus Powder

Directions
1. Make the lime syrup by heating 3 tablespoons of sugar and the juice of 3 limes in saucepan over a medium heat
2. Stir until the sugar dissolves and set aside to cool
3. Mix the cornstarch and with 2 tablespoons of milk to make a paste
4. Mix the remaining milk with the heavy cream, remaining sugar, corn syrup, and lime zest in a saucepan and bring to the boil and stir until the sugar dissolves
5. Remove from the heat and mix in the cornstarch
6. Return to the heat and stir until thickened
7. Pour into the cream cheese and whisk vigorously until smooth
8. Mix in the yogurt, lime syrup and dried hibiscus powder
9. Chill in the refrigerator for 20 minutes
10. Pour into an ice cream maker and process according to the directions for frozen yogurt
11. Freeze for 4 hours before serving

GRAPEFRUIT FROZEN YOGURT

A zesty, tart, and slightly sweet frozen yogurt that is reminiscent of a grapefruit sorbet but with a creamy base and crisp tang of Greek yogurt.

Makes: 6 Serves
Prep: 5 minutes plus 4 hours freezing time

Ingredients:
2 Cups Greek Yogurt
2/3 Cup Grapefruit Juice
3/4 Cup Sugar
1 Cup Heavy Cream
1 Tbsp Grapefruit Zest

Directions
1. Mix all the ingredients together in a large bowl until smooth
2. Place in an ice cream maker and follow the directions for frozen yogurt
3. Freeze for 4 hours before serving

EARL GREY TEA FROZEN YOGURT

Enjoy this refined recipe that uses the subtle smoky flavors of Earl Grey Tea to make a creamy yet sharp frozen yogurt recipe.

Makes: 8 Serves
Prep: 5 minutes plus 4 hours freezing time

Ingredients:
3 ¾ Cups Greek Yogurt
6oz Earl Grey Tea, brewed and chilled
1/3 Cup Honey
1/4 Tsp Salt

Directions
1. In a bowl, whisk together the Greek yogurt, tea, honey, and salt
2. Pour into an ice cream maker and follow the instructions for frozen yogurt
3. Freeze for 4 hours before serving

HONEY-BANANA FROZEN YOGURT

A healthier alternative to ice cream that uses honey and the natural sugars found in bananas, this recipe focuses on a tried and tested flavor combination mixed with yogurt to make a sweet yet tart dessert.

Makes: 8 Serves
Prep: 10 minutes plus 4 hours freezing time

Ingredients:
1 ¼ Cups Greek Yogurt
4 Bananas
2 Tbsps Honey
1 Tbsp Lemon Juice
1/2 Tsp Cinnamon

Directions
1. Puree the bananas, honey, lemon juice, and cinnamon in a blender until smooth
2. In a large bowl, mix in the yogurt and stir well
3. Freeze until solid then puree in a blender
4. Freeze again for 4 hours before serving

KEY LIME PIE FROZEN YOGURT

This delicious lime frozen yogurt is transformed into a taste of key lime pie with the clever addition of graham crackers and whipped cream.

Makes: 8 Serves
Prep: 5 minutes plus 4 hours freezing time

Ingredients:
3 Cups Greek Yogurt
14oz Can Condensed Milk
1 Cup Lime Juice
Zest of 1 Lime
1 Tsp Vanilla Extract

For the Garnish:
Graham Cracker Crumbs
Whipped Cream

Directions
1. In a bowl whisk together all the ingredients until well combined
2. Pour into an ice cream maker and follow the directions for frozen yogurt
3. Freeze for 4 hours before serving
4. Serve with graham cracker crumbs and whipped cream on top

CLEMENTINE FROZEN YOGURT

A sweeter take on an orange frozen yogurt recipe with the use of clementine juice. Enjoy these 'winter oranges' to make a sweet treat that is healthier than typical ice cream.

Makes: 8 Serves
Prep: 5 minutes plus 4 hours freezing time

Ingredients:
2 Cups Greek Yogurt
2/3 Cup Clementine Juice
1 Tbsp Clementine Zest
1 Cup Heavy Cream
1/3 Cup Sugar

Directions
1. In a bowl whisk together all the ingredients until the sugar dissolves and no longer feels grainy
2. Put the mix into an ice cream maker and process according to the instructions for frozen yogurt
3. Freeze for 4 hours before serving

CREAMED CORN FROZEN YOGURT

Corn is often considered a savory food item but it is perfect in a sweet dessert like this delicious corn frozen yogurt recipe.

Makes: 8 Serves
Prep: 20 minutes plus 8 hours chilling time and 4 hours freezing time

Ingredients:
2 Cups Greek Yogurt
4 Ears of Corn
2 ¼ Cups Milk
1/2 Cup Sugar
1 Sheet Gelatin
1 Tsp Vanilla Extract
1/4 Cup Corn Syrup

Directions
1. Cut the kernels from the corn and place in a blender with 1/2 cup of milk and blitz until smooth
2. In a saucepan over a low heat mix the corn mixture, the remaining milk, sugar, and gelatin until the gelatin has dissolved
3. Pass the mixture through a strainer to remove any remaining pieces of corn
4. Cool then mix in the vanilla extract, yogurt, and corn syrup
5. Chill for 8 hours
6. Pour into an ice cream maker and follow the directions for frozen yogurt
7. Freeze for 4 hours before serving

ALMOND FROZEN YOGURT

This recipe uses the subtle nutty flavors of almonds combined with delicious fruity honey to make a refined and flavorful dessert.

Makes: 10 Serves
Prep: 5 minutes plus 4 hours freezing time

Ingredients:
4 Cups Greek Yogurt
1/3 Cup Sugar
5 Tbsps Honey
1/3 Cup Almonds, sliced
1 Tsp Almond Extract

Directions
1. Mix the yogurt, sugar, honey and almond extract in a large bowl
2. Scatter over the sliced almonds and fold to combine
3. Place in an ice cream maker and process according to the instructions for frozen yogurt
4. Freeze for 4 hours before serving

RHUBARB-STRAWBERRY FROZEN YOGURT

Mighty rhubarb is used in this recipe to make a pretty pink frozen yogurt that also uses sweet and tart strawberries for a perfect balance of flavors.

Makes: 8 Serves
Prep: 20 minutes plus 4 hours freezing time

Ingredients:
4 Cups Whole Milk Yogurt
1/2 Cup Sugar
3 Tbsps Honey
1 ½ Cups Strawberries, sliced
1/2 Cup Rhubarb
1 Tsp Lemon Juice
1 Tsp Sugar
1 Tsp Cornstarch

Directions
1. Cook the rhubarb and strawberries in a splash of water over a high heat until softened
2. Add the cornstarch, 1 teaspoon of sugar and lemon juice and stir until thickened then remove from the heat
3. Set aside to cool
4. In a bowl mix the yogurt, sugar and honey until no longer grainy
5. Transfer to an ice cream maker and process using the directions for frozen yogurt
6. Transfer the frozen yogurt to a freezer-proof container and ripple through the rhubarb and strawberry sauce
7. Freeze for 4 hours before serving

SALTED CARAMEL FROZEN YOGURT

This clever recipe uses a simple jam jar to make this caramel frozen yogurt, without the need for any fancy kitchen equipment.

Makes: 8 Serves
Prep: 20 minutes plus 4 hours freezing time

Ingredients:
2 Cups Greek Yogurt
2/3 Cup Sugar
1 Tbsp Water
1/4 Cup Milk
1 Tsp Vanilla
1/4 Tsp Sea Salt

Directions
1. Make the caramel by stirring the sugar and water consistently over a high heat until the mixture turns amber in color
2. Remove and add the milk, stirring constantly as the mixture will bubble and splutter
3. Once the mixture has come together into a smooth sauce, set aside to cool
4. Put the yogurt in a jam jar and mix with 1/3 of the caramel sauce
5. Add the vanilla, salt and remaining sauce and store again until incorporated
6. Cover the top of the jar and place in the freezer for 4 hours, removing every 30 minutes to whisk and break up the ice crystals
7. Serve as desired

APPLE PIE FROZEN YOGURT

Enjoy all the traditional flavors of comforting apple pie in this clever recipe that transforms them into frozen yogurt form.

Makes: 6 Serves
Prep: 10 minutes plus 5 hours freezing time

Ingredients:
1 Cup Greek Yogurt
1 ½ Tsps Apple Cider
1/4 Tsp Vanilla Extract
1/2 Tsp Honey
1/4 Tsp Cinnamon
1/4 Cup Apples, diced
1/4 Cup Lemon Juice
Pinch of Cinnamon
Pinch of Brown Sugar

Directions
1. Mix yogurt, apple cider, vanilla extract, honey, and ¼ teaspoon of cinnamon in a freezer-safe container and place in the freezer for 1 hour
2. Mix apples, lemon juice, pinch of cinnamon, and brown sugar in a bowl and set aside
3. Remove frozen yogurt mix from the freezer and whisk to loosen
4. Stir in apple mixture and return to the freezer for 4 hours
5. Serve as desired

LEMON-BASIL FROZEN YOGURT

People might not think that herbal basil is a natural addition to frozen yogurt, but actually it is delicious mixed with tart lemon zest and a sweet frozen yogurt base.

Makes: 8 Serves
Prep: 5 minutes plus 4 hours freezing time

Ingredients:
6 Cups Greek Yogurt
1 Cup Basil Leaves, chopped finely
1/2 Cup Sugar
1/2 Chopped Walnuts
4 Tbsps Lemon Zest

Directions
1. Mix yogurt, basil, sugar, walnuts, and lemon peel in a bowl until smooth
2. Pour into an ice cream maker and mix according to the instructions for frozen yoghurt
3. Freeze for 4 hours before serving

BLACK SESAME FROZEN YOGURT

The black sesame seeds in this recipe add a nutty flavor that is cut with the sweet honey to make a different yet delicious frozen yogurt sweet treat.

Makes: 6 Serves
Prep: 20 minutes plus 4 hours freezing time

Ingredients:
2 Cups Greek Yogurt
3 Tbsps Black Sesame Seeds
2 Tbsps Honey

Directions
1. In a frying pan over a medium heat dry fry the sesame seeds for 3 minutes
2. Place in a spice grinder or pestle and mortar and grind to a paste
3. In a bowl mix the paste with the yogurt and honey
4. Pour mix into an ice cream maker and follow the instructions for frozen yogurt
5. Freeze for 4 hours and then serve

CARROT-CINNAMON FROZEN YOGURT

With a mix of carrots and cinnamon, this frozen yogurt captures all the delicious flavors of carrot cake without the heavy consistency.

Makes: 8 Serves
Prep: 20 minutes plus 4 hours freezing time

Ingredients:
2 Cups Greek Yogurt
1 Cup Carrot Juice
3/4 Cup Maple Syrup
1 Tsp Vanilla Extract
1/2 Tsp Cinnamon

Directions
1. Blend all the ingredients in a blender until smooth
2. Transfer to an ice cream maker and follow the directions for frozen yogurt
3. Freeze for 4 hours before serving

GINGERBREAD FROZEN YOGURT

A fabulous frozen yogurt recipe for the holidays that uses spices to replicate the taste of Christmassy gingerbread.

Makes: 8 Servings
Prep: 30 minutes plus 3 hours freezing time

Ingredients:
2 Cups Greek Yogurt
1/2 Cup Milk
1/4 Molasses
1/3 Brown Sugar
2 Tbsps Fresh Ginger, grated
1 Tsp Cinnamon
1/4 Tsp Black Pepper
1/4 Cup Water
1/2 Sugar
2 Egg Whites
1 Tsp Vanilla Extract

Directions
1. Place the milk, molasses, brown sugar, ginger, cinnamon, and pepper in a saucepan over a medium heat and stir until the sugar dissolves
2. Remove from the heat and leave to cool. Then strain and set aside
3. Boil the sugar and water in a saucepan over a medium heat without stirring for 1 minute
4. Beat the egg whites until soft peaks form and then pour in the sugar syrup in a continuous stream, whisking constantly
5. Whisk for 2 minutes until glossy
6. In a separate bowl whisk the yogurt, vanilla, and milk mixture until smooth
7. Gently fold in the meringue
8. Transfer to an ice cream maker and process according to the directions for frozen yogurt

9. Freeze for 3 hours before serving

BERRY AND CUSTARD FROZEN YOGURT

The traditional dessert of berries and custard is given a makeover in this frozen yogurt version of this classic flavor combination.

Makes: 8 Servings
Prep: 20 minutes plus 12 hours freezing time

Ingredients:
4 Cups Greek Yogurt
1 ½ Cups Vanilla Custard
1 Cup Confectioner's Sugar
1 Tsp Vanilla Essence
1 Punnet Strawberries
1 Punnet Raspberries

Directions
1. Whisk the yogurt, custard, and vanilla in a bowl until well combined
2. Freeze for 6 hours
3. Blend the berries and sugar in a blender until they form a puree and then place in the fridge to chill
4. Blend the yogurt mixture in a blender until creamy and then fold in the berry sauce
5. Freeze for 6 hours before serving

DOUBLE CHOCOLATE CHIP FROZEN YOGURT

Enjoy a lighter version of double chocolate chip ice cream with this frozen yogurt recipe that celebrates chocolate in all its forms!

Makes: 8 Serves
Prep: 20 minutes plus 4 hours freezing time

Ingredients:
4 Cups Greek Yogurt
1/2 Cup Almond Milk
1/2 Cup Chocolate Powder
2/3 Cup Sugar
1 Tsp Vanilla Essence
2 Cups Chocolate Chips

Directions
1. Place all the ingredients in a blender except the chocolate chips and blend until smooth
2. Pour into an ice cream maker and follow the instructions for frozen yogurt
3. Place in a freezer-safe container and fold in the chocolate chips
4. Freeze for 4 hours before serving

LYCHEE FROZEN YOGURT

This recipe uses the fruity and floral flavors of lychees with their natural syrup to make a sweet treat that is as refreshing as it is delicious.

Makes: 8 Serves
Prep: 10 minutes plus 3 hours freezing time

Ingredients:
2 Cups Greek Yogurt
2/3 Cup Heavy Cream
2/3 Cup Sugar
1 Can of Lychees

Directions
1. Place the lychee fruit in a blender, reserving the syrup for later
2. Add the yogurt and sugar and blend until smooth
3. Add the cream and syrup and blend again
4. Pour into an ice cream maker and follow the directions for frozen yogurt
5. Freeze for 3 hours before serving

FROZEN MARGHERITA FROZEN YOGURT

Who says you can't enjoy a frozen Margherita for dessert? Well now you can with this canny twist on the classic cocktail.

Makes: 8 Serves
Prep: 5 minutes plus 4 hours freezing time

Ingredients:
3 Cups Greek Yogurt
1/2 Cup Lime Juice
4 Tbsps Agave Syrup
4 Tbsps Tequila

Directions
1. Mix the yogurt, lime juice, and agave syrup together in a bowl
2. Transfer to an ice cream maker and mix for 5 minutes according to the directions for frozen yogurt
3. Add the tequila
4. Continue to churn according to the directions for frozen yogurt
5. Freeze for 4 hours before serving

KIWI FROZEN YOGURT

This frozen yogurt takes on a gorgeous pale green hue thanks to the delicate flesh of the kiwis and finds the perfect balance between sweet and tart.

Makes: 8 Serves
Prep: 5 minutes plus 4 hours freezing time

Ingredients:
3 Cups Greek Yogurt
4 Kiwis
1/2 Cup Sugar

Directions
1. Blend the kiwi flesh, yogurt, and sugar in a blender until smooth
2. Pour into an ice cream maker and follow the directions for frozen yogurt
3. Freeze for 4 hours before serving

RICOTTA AND ORANGE FROZEN YOGURT

Switch up classic frozen yogurt with the addition of some tangy ricotta that gives it a fuller and more sophisticated flavor. This recipe adds orange zest to round out the flavors.

Makes: 8 Serves
Prep: 5 minutes plus 4 hours freezing time

Ingredients:
3 Cups Greek Yogurt
1/4 Cup Ricotta
Zest of 1 Orange
3/4 Cup Sugar
1/4 Tsp Salt

Directions
1. Mix all the ingredients in a bowl until smooth
2. Transfer to an ice cream maker and follow the instructions for frozen yogurt
3. Freeze for 4 hours before serving

EASY STRAWBERRY JAM FROZEN YOGURT

Skip a few steps by using jam to flavor your frozen yogurt with this clever little recipe. This dessert uses strawberry jam but you could use any flavor of preserve you please.

Makes: 10 Serves
Prep: 5 minutes plus 4 hours freezing time

Ingredients:
3 Cups Greek Yogurt
1 Pint Strawberry Jam
2 Tbsps Balsamic Vinegar
1 Tbsp Corn Syrup

Directions
1. Place all the ingredients in a bowl and stir until smooth
2. Transfer to an ice cream maker and process using the directions for frozen yogurt
3. Freeze for 4 hours before serving

MAPLE AND RUM FROZEN YOGURT

Maple and rum are a perfect combination that work amazingly well in a frozen yogurt recipe, producing a creamy result that doesn't use any unhealthy sugar.

Makes: 8 Serves
Prep: 5 minutes plus 4 hours freezing time

Ingredients:
2 Cups Greek Yogurt
1/2 Cup Heavy Cream
1/2 Cup Maple Syrup
1 Tsp Vanilla Extract
1 Tbsp Rum

Directions
1. Whisk together all the ingredients in a bowl until smooth
2. Transfer to an ice cream maker and follow the directions for frozen yogurt
3. Freeze for 4 hours before serving

RED VELVET FROZEN YOGURT

This frozen yogurt recipe incorporates red velvet batter with a frozen yogurt base that makes a delicious dessert that is not as heavy as the cake variety.

Makes: 12 Serves
Prep: 30 minutes plus 4 hours freezing time

Ingredients:
1/4 Cup Butter, melted
1/2 Cup Sugar
1/4 Cup Brown Sugar
1/2 Cup Flour
1/4 Cup Cocoa Powder
Pinch of Salt
2 Tbsps Cream Cheese
2 Cups Greek Yogurt
2 Tbsps Red Food Coloring
1/3 Cup Chocolate Chips

For the Cream Cheese Mixture:
8oz Cream Cheese
1 Cup Greek Yogurt
1/4 Cup Sugar
1/2 Tsp Vanilla Bean Paste

Directions
1. Mix the butter and sugars in a bowl until creamy
2. Sift in the flour, salt, and cocoa powder and whisk well
3. Mix in the cream cheese, yogurt, and red food coloring and beat to combine
4. Fold in the chocolate chips
5. Pour into a loaf tin lined with baking parchment and set aside
6. Make the cream cheese mixture by mixing the cream cheese, yogurt, and vanilla paste

7. Pour on top of the red mixture in the loaf tin and swirl through
8. Freeze for 4 hours before serving

CHOCOLATE HAZELNUT FROZEN YOGURT

Make this easy yet decedent dessert using chocolate hazelnut spread to give it a full bodied flavor that tastes more like ice cream rather than leaner frozen yogurt.

Makes: 8 Serves
Prep: 5 minutes plus 3 hours freezing time

Ingredients:
2 Cups Greek Yogurt
2/3 Cup Chocolate Hazelnut Spread
1 Tsp Vanilla Extract
1/4 Tsp Salt
1/4 Cup Cocoa Powder
1/3 Cup Sugar
1 Cup Milk

Directions
1. Place all the ingredients in a blender and blitz until smooth
2. Transfer to an ice cream maker and follow the directions for frozen yogurt
3. Freeze for 3 hours before serving

BROWNIE BATTER FROZEN YOGURT

What's better than a brownie to cure that sweets craving? How about brownie batter frozen yogurt that is easy and quick to make but tastes exactly like the real deal.

Makes: 8 Serves
Prep: 5 minutes plus 4 hours freezing time

Ingredients:
3 Cups Greek Yogurt
1/4 Cup Cocoa powder
1/8 Tsp Baking Soda
1/4 Tsp Salt
1 Tsp Vanilla Extract
4 Tbsps Sugar
2 Tbsps Brown Sugar

Directions
1. Whisk all the ingredients together in a bowl until well mixed
2. Transfer to an ice cream maker and process using the directions for frozen yogurt
3. Freeze for 4 hours before serving

MOJITO FROZEN YOGURT

Enjoy your favorite cocktail in a whole different way with this mojito-inspired frozen yogurt recipe.

Makes: 8 Serves
Prep: 20 minutes plus 4 hours freezing time

Ingredients:
1/2oz Mint Leaves
1 Cup Milk
1/2 Tsp Xantham Gun
1 Tsp Arrowroot Starch
1/4 Cup Sugar
2 Eggs
2 Cups Greek Yogurt
Juice of 1 lime
Zest of 1 lime
2oz Light Rum
1 Tbsp Fresh Mint, chopped

Directions
1. Bring the milk to the boil in a saucepan over a medium heat and add the mint leaves
2. Take off the heat and leave to steep for 30 minutes
3. Strain and set aside to cool
4. In a bowl, mix the arrowroot starch with 2 tablespoons of the milk and stir until dissolved
5. In a separate bowl mix the remaining milk with the xantham gum and sugar until no longer grainy
6. Whisk the eggs in a bowl and stir in the milk mixture
7. Place in a saucepan over a medium heat and stir until thickened
8. Put the yogurt in a bowl and mix in the milk and eggs followed by all the other ingredients
9. Pour into an ice cream maker and follow the directions for frozen yogurt

10. Freeze for 4 hours before serving scattered with the remaining mint leaves

PASSION FRUIT FROZEN YOGURT

This pleasingly light frozen yogurt recipe uses passion fruit pulp to create a pretty orange dessert that hits all the right sweet and sour nights.

Makes: 8 Serves
Prep: 5 minutes plus 4 hours freezing time

Ingredients:
3 Cups Greek Yogurt
3/4 Cup Sugar
1 Tsp Vanilla Essence
6 Tbsps Passion Fruit Pulp

Directions
1. Place all the ingredients in a bowl and stir until smooth
2. Transfer to an ice cream maker and process using the directions for frozen yogurt
3. Freeze for 4 hours before serving
4. Serve scattered with passion fruit seeds as desired

LEMON MERINGUE FROZEN YOGURT

This fancy recipe incorporates fluffy homemade meringue with zesty lemon frozen yoghurt to make a delightful play on a traditional lemon meringue pie.

Makes: 8 Serves
Prep: 20 minutes plus 4 hours freezing time

Ingredients:
2 Cups Greek Yogurt
1 Tsp Arrowroot Starch
1 Tsp Gelatin
1 Cup Milk
2 Eggs, separated
2 Tbsps Lemon Juice
1 Tsp Lemon Zest
1/3 Cup Agave Nectar

Directions
1. Place the gelatin in a bowl and stir in two tablespoons of milk
2. In a separate bowl add the arrowroot and 2 tablespoons of milk and stir
3. Set aside both bowls
4. Whisk together the egg yolks and remaining milk in a saucepan over a low heat until frothy then add the gelatin until dissolved
5. Stir in the arrowroot for 1 minute and then remove from the heat
6. Set aside to cool
7. In a bowl, mix the yogurt, lemon juice, lemon zest and agave
8. Stir the cooled egg mixture into the yogurt until well mixed
9. Whip the egg whites to form soft peaks and fold into the yogurt mixture

10. Place in an ice cream maker and follow the instructions for frozen yogurt
11. Freeze for 4 hours before serving

FIG FROZEN YOGURT

Make a deliciously tasty yet healthy dessert by combining fresh figs with honey to make this pretty pink hued frozen yogurt.

Makes: 8 Serves
Prep: 10 minutes plus 4 hours freezing time

Ingredients:
2 Cups Greek Yogurt
4 Cups Figs
1/3 Cup Honey
Juice of 1/2 Lemon

Directions
1. Place the figs, honey and lemon juice in a blender and pulse until smooth
2. Transfer to a bowl and mix in the yogurt
3. Transfer to an ice cream maker and process using the directions for frozen yogurt
4. Freeze for 4 hours before serving

BLACKCURRANT FROZEN YOGURT

In recent years blackcurrant frozen yogurt has developed quite a following to rival classic vanilla. See what all the fuss is about with this version you can make yourself.

Makes: 8 Serves
Prep: 10 minutes plus 4 hours freezing time

Ingredients:
3 Cups Greek Yogurt
2/3 Cup Sugar
6oz Blackcurrants
1/3 Cup Water

Directions
1. Place the blackcurrants in a saucepan over a medium heat and add the water and sugar and simmer until softened
2. Pass the mixture through a sieve
3. Mix the blackcurrant juice with the yogurt in a bowl
4. Pour into an ice cream maker and follow the directions for frozen yogurt
5. Freeze for 4 hours before serving

CHAMOMILE FROZEN YOGURT

This delightful recipe is made using lightly flavored chamomile flowers that delicately perfume the frozen yogurt making a refined and fragrant dessert.

Makes: 8 Serves
Prep: 20 minutes plus 4 hours freezing time

Ingredients:
3 Cups Greek Yogurt
2 Tbsps Chamomile Flowers
2 Cups Coconut Milk
1 Tsp Arrowroot
2 Tsps Vanilla Extract
1/2 Cup Honey

Directions
1. Place the arrowroot in a bowl and stir in 1/4 cup of coconut milk until smooth
2. Bring to the boil and whisk in the remaining coconut milk
3. Remove from the head and add the chamomile flowers and leave to steep for 10 minutes
4. Strain and discard the flowers
5. Whisk the yogurt, vanilla and honey into the milk mixture until smooth
6. Pour into an ice cream maker and follow the directions for frozen yogurt
7. Freeze for 4 hours before serving

DATE AND HONEY FROZEN YOGURT

The frozen yogurt version of a power packed date and honey shake. It's naturally sweet, full of nutrients, and creamy on the palette.

Makes: 6 Serves
Prep: 5 minutes plus 4 hours freezing time

Ingredients:
1/3 Cup Dates, minced
2/3 Cup Honey
1/3 Cup Evaporated Milk
1 Tbsp Gelatin
2 Cups Greek Yogurt

Directions
1. Place the minced dates and honey in a bowl and mix
2. Heat the milk in a saucepan over a medium heat and add the gelatin and date mixture
3. Stir until the gelatin has dissolved
4. Remove from the heat and leave to cool
5. In a bowl whisk the yoghurt then slowly add the milk mixture and stir to combine
6. Pour into an ice cream maker and follow the directions for frozen yogurt
7. Freeze for 4 hours before serving

GREEN APPLE FROZEN YOGURT

If you like a really tart and refreshing frozen yogurt, then look no further than this tasty green apple recipe that is so light it almost resembles a sorbet.

Makes: 6 Serves
Prep: 5 minutes plus 4 hours freezing time

Ingredients:
2 Cups Greek Yogurt
2 Green Apples
3 Tbsps Sugar Syrup

Directions
1. Place the apples in a blender with the yogurt and sugar syrup and puree until smooth
2. Transfer to an ice cream maker and follow the directions for frozen yogurt
3. Freeze for 4 hours before serving

TIRAMISU FROZEN YOGURT

If you love Tiramisu but fancy something cooler for summer, then try this frozen yogurt version that uses all the classic flavors to create a devilishly delicious dessert.

Makes: 5 Serves
Prep: 15 minutes plus 8 hours freezing time

Ingredients:
1 Cup Greek Yogurt
1 Tbsp Cocoa Powder
2 Tbsps Brown Sugar
1 Tbsp Kahlua
1/2 Tsp Instant Coffee
1 Tsp Water

Directions
1. In a bowl, combine the yogurt, cocoa powder, brown sugar, and Kahlua
2. Mix the instant coffee with water until dissolved and then add to the mixture
3. Stir in the yogurt until well combined
4. Place in the freezer for 8 hours, stirring every few hours to break up any ice crystals
5. Serve as desired

FUDGE FROZEN YOGURT POPS

As summer gets underway, why not whip up a batch of these easy to make fudge popsicles that are heavy on flavor but light on the palette.

Makes: 6 Serves
Prep: 10 minutes plus 5 hours freezing time

Ingredients:
1 Cup Greek Yogurt
1 ½ Cups Milk
1/3 Cup Unsweetened Cocoa Powder
2 Tbsps Sugar
1 Tsp Vanilla Essence
8oz Chocolate Chips
Pinch of Salt

Directions
1. In a saucepan over a medium heat mix the cocoa powder, sugar, vanilla, and salt
2. Whisk constantly and simmer for 5 minutes
3. Pour the warm mixture into a bowl containing the chocolate chips and mix until dissolved
4. Leave to cool slightly and then mix in the yogurt
5. Once completely cooled, pour into popsicle molds
6. Freeze for 5 hours before serving

BUTTER PECAN FROZEN YOGURT

A lighter version of butter pecan ice cream that retains all of the classic flavors mixed with zingy yogurt for added freshness.

Makes: 8 Serves
Prep: 5 minutes plus 4 hours freezing time

Ingredients:
2 Cups Greek Yogurt
3 Tbsps Butter
2 Eggs
1/2 Cup Honey
1/2 Cup Chopped Pecans
1/2 Tsp Cinnamon
1 Tsp Vanilla

Directions
1. Mix the pecans, cinnamon and 2 tablespoons of butter in a pan over a medium heat
2. Cook until the butter is melted and the pecans have lightly colored. Remove and set aside
3. In a bowl, mix together the yogurt, eggs and honey until smooth
4. Transfer to a saucepan over a low heat and add the pecan mixture and 1 tablespoon of butter
5. Heat gently for 2 minutes stirring continuously
6. Remove from the heat and stir in the vanilla essence
7. Transfer to an ice cream maker and process using the directions for frozen yogurt
8. Freeze for 4 hours before serving

TANGY TOMATO FROZEN YOGURT

The perfect recipe if you have ripe tomatoes to use up as their acidity is the perfect match for a hit of sweetness and a scoop of yogurt.

Makes: 3 Serves
Prep: 5 minutes plus 4 hours freezing time

Ingredients:
1 Cup Greek Yogurt
1 Heirloom Tomato
1/4 Cup Sugar

Directions
1. Place all the ingredients in a blender and blitz until smooth
2. Transfer to an ice cream maker and process using the directions for frozen yogurt
3. Freeze for 4 hours before serving

COOKIES AND CREAM FROZEN YOGURT

Enjoy the classic taste of cookies and cream but with a lighter finish with this frozen yogurt recipe that uses less sugar than normal ice cream.

Makes: 8 Serves
Prep: 5 minutes plus 4 hours freezing time

Ingredients:
3 Cups Greek Yogurt
1/3 Cup Sugar
1/2 Tbsp Vanilla Paste
8 Cookies, chopped

Directions
1. Mix yogurt, sugar and vanilla paste in a bowl until the sugar is dissolved
2. Place in an ice cream maker and follow the directions for frozen yogurt
3. Transfer to a freezer-safe container and fold in the chopped cookies
4. Freeze for 4 hours before serving

BLACK PEPPER FROZEN YOGURT

If you want to try something a little out of the ordinary, then don't be afraid to mix black pepper with a basic frozen yogurt recipe. This mix of slightly piquant pepper and sugary caramel is delicious.

Makes: 8 Serves
Prep: 15 minutes plus 4 hours freezing time

Ingredients:
2 Cups Greek Yogurt
1 Cup Sugar
2 Tsps Cornstarch
2 Tsps Ground Black Pepper
1 ½ Cups Whole Milk

Directions
1. Place the sugar and pepper in a saucepan over a medium heat
2. Do not stir but swirl the pan until the sugar melts and turns amber
3. Remove from the heat
4. Whisk the cornstarch and milk together and add to the caramel sauce
5. Add a pinch of salt and swirl in the pan until well mixed
6. Leave to cool slightly then stir in the yogurt
7. Transfer to an ice cream maker and process using the directions for frozen yogurt
8. Freeze for 4 hours before serving

MOCHA FROZEN YOGURT

This clever mocha frozen yogurt recipe uses chocolate milk and instant coffee to replicate the flavors of the classic drink.

Makes: 8 Servings
Prep: 5 minutes plus 4 hours freezing time

Ingredients:
2 Cups Vanilla Greek Yogurt
1 Pint Chocolate Milk
2 Tsps Cocoa Powder
1 Tbsp Instant Coffee
1/4 Cup Sugar

Directions
1. Place all the ingredients in a bowl and whisk until well mixed
2. Transfer to an ice cream maker and process using the directions for frozen yogurt
3. Freeze for 4 hours before serving

SWEET POTATO FROZEN YOGURT POPSICLES

Try this healthy frozen yogurt that uses the natural sugars of sweet potatoes to make these sunshine yellow popsicles that will be sure to put a smile on your face.

Makes: 8 Servings
Prep: 5 minutes plus 4 hours freezing time

Ingredients:
2 Cups Honey Greek Yogurt
1 Cup Sweet Potatoes, mashed
1/4 Cup Milk
Pinch of Cinnamon

Directions
1. Place all the ingredients in a food processor and blitz until smooth
2. Transfer to an ice cream maker and follow the direction for frozen yogurt
3. Freeze for 4 hours before serving

GUAVA FROZEN YOGURT

Harness the delicious sweetness of guava fruit with this simple yet delightful frozen yogurt recipe.

Makes: 6 Serves
Prep: 5 minutes plus 4 hours freezing time

Ingredients:
2 Cups Greek Yogurt
1 Cup Guava
1/3 Cup Honey
1/4 Cup Milk
1 Tsp Vanilla Extract

Directions
1. Place all the ingredients in a food processor and blitz until smooth
2. Transfer to an ice cream maker and follow the instructions for frozen yogurt
3. Freeze for 4 hours before serving

LEMONADE FROZEN YOGURT

Take a trip back to childhood with this gorgeous recipe for lemonade frozen yogurt. This recipe uses lemonade concentrate to bring out the big kid in you and is perfect for youngsters in the kitchen.

Makes: 10 Serves
Prep: 5 minutes plus 2 hours freezing time

Ingredients:
1 Quart Greek Yogurt
12oz Lemonade Concentrate
1 Cup Milk
1/4 Cup Lemon Juice
1/2 Cup Sugar

Directions
1. Whisk all the ingredients together until smooth
2. Transfer to an ice cream maker and follow the directions for frozen yogurt
3. Freeze for 3 hours before serving

GRAPE FROZEN YOGURT

If you have a glut of grapes then this recipe is perfect for using them up. It's simple and refreshing and so easy you don't even have to peel the fruit!

Makes: 8 Servings
Prep: 5 minutes plus 4 hours freezing time

Ingredients:
3 Cups Greek Yogurt
1 Cup Grapes
1/2 Cup Sugar

Directions
1. Place all the ingredients in a blender and blend until a puree forms
2. Transfer to an ice cream maker and follow the directions for frozen yogurt
3. Freeze for at least 4 hours

HONEYCOMB FROZEN YOGURT

This recipe uses chunks of honeycomb mixed with basic vanilla yogurt to make a delightfully crunchy yet creamy dessert.

Makes: 6 Servings
Prep: 10 minutes plus 4 hours freezing time

Ingredients:
1 Cup Greek Yogurt
1 Cup Condensed Milk
2/3 Cream Cheese
1 Tsp Vanilla Extract
1/4 Cup Orange Juice
1/2 Cup Chocolate Coated Honeycomb

Directions
1. Stir the cream cheese, condensed milk, vanilla, lemon juice and yogurt together in a bowl
2. Crush the chocolate honeycomb into small pieces and stir into the yogurt mixture
3. Place the mixture into an ice cream maker and follow the instructions for frozen yogurt
4. Freeze for 4 hours before serving sprinkled with extra honeycomb

CHOCOLATE MALT FROZEN YOGURT

If you like malted milk, then you will love this delicately flavored frozen yogurt ice cream that mixes malt and chocolate milk to make a creamy and subtle dessert.

Makes: 8 Serves
Prep: 5 minutes plus 4 hours freezing time

Ingredients:
4 Cups Vanilla Greek Yogurt
1 Cup Chocolate Milk
1/4 Cup Malted Milk

Directions
1. Place all the ingredients in a blender and blend until well combined
2. Transfer to an ice cream maker and follow the instructions for frozen yogurt
3. Freeze for at least 4 hours before serving

SPEEDY PAPAYA FROZEN YOGURT

This Asian fruit becomes the star of the show in this quick recipe that can be thrown together in minutes. Perfect for when you have a sudden craving for healthy frozen yogurt.

Makes: 2 Serves
Prep: 10 minutes

Ingredients:
1 Cup Greek Yogurt
1 Cup Frozen Papaya, chopped
1 Tsp Lime Juice
1 Tbsp Honey

Directions
1. Place all the ingredients in a food processor and pulse until smooth and creamy
2. Serve immediately

VANILLA BOURBON FROZEN YOGURT

Enjoy this grown up version of simple vanilla frozen yogurt with the addition of some bourbon that goes perfectly with heavy cream to make a sweet treat with a bit of a kick.

Makes: 6 Servings
Prep: 15 minutes plus 2 hours freezing time

Ingredients:
1 Cup Greek Yogurt
1 Cup Heavy Cream
1/2 Vanilla Bean
1/2 Cup Cane Sugar
3 Tbsps Bourbon Whisky

Directions
1. Place the sugar, cream and vanilla in a saucepan over a medium heat and stir until the sugar is dissolved
2. Set aside and leave the vanilla pod to steep for 20 minutes
3. Place the yogurt in a separate bowl and strain in the cream mixture
4. Whisk until well mixed and then stir in the bourbon
5. Place in an ice cream maker and follow the directions for frozen yogurt
6. Freeze for 2 hours before serving

POMEGRANATE FROZEN YOGURT

A tart and tangy frozen yogurt recipe that is full of all the health benefits of powerful pomegranates.

Makes: 5 Serves
Prep: 5 minutes plus 4 hours freezing time

Ingredients:
1 Cup Greek Yogurt
1/2 Cup Milk
1/2 Cup Sugar
3 Tbsps Pomegranate Juice
3 Tbsps Honey

Directions
1. Place all the ingredients mixing bowl and beat until smooth
2. Transfer to an ice cream maker and follow the directions for frozen yogurt
3. Freeze for 4 hours before serving

NO SUGAR FROZEN YOGURT

If you want a no sugar version of frozen yogurt that is also gluten free then try this easy recipe. It can also be made fat free if you use a non-fat yogurt.

Makes: 8 Serves
Prep: 2 hours and 5 minutes plus 4 hours freezing time

Ingredients:
4 Cups Non-fat Greek Yogurt
1 Tsp Vanilla Bean Paste
1/2 Cup Stevia Sugar Free Syrup

Directions
1. Strain the yogurt over a bowl for 2 hours to remove the excess liquid
2. In a bowl mix the drained yogurt, the vanilla, and the stevia
3. Transfer to an ice cream maker and process according to the instructions for frozen yogurt
4. Freeze for 4 hours before serving

RED BEAN FROZEN YOGURT ICY POPS

A popular dessert item in Asia, red beans make a bright, sweet, and earthy addition to this frozen dessert. You also only need three ingredients for this sweet treat!

Makes: 2 Serves
Prep: 5 minutes plus 3 hours freezing time

Ingredients:
6oz Plain Yogurt
3oz Red Beans
1 Tbsp Honey

Directions
1. Mix all the ingredients in a bowl until well mixed
2. Pour into popsicle molds and freeze for 3 hours before serving

MELON FROZEN YOGURT POPSICLES

These popsicles couldn't be easier to make as they use molds so that you don't need to spend time churning the mix in an ice cream maker. A perky burst of melon adds to the refreshing and sweet flavor.

Makes: 8 Serves
Prep: 5 minutes plus 4 hours freezing time

Ingredients:
2 Cups Greek Yogurt
3 Cups Melon, cubed
1 Cup Honey

Directions
1. Place the melon in a blender and blitz until it forms a puree
2. Transfer to a bowl and mix with the yogurt and honey until well combined
3. Pour into popsicle molds and freeze for at least 4 hours

ROSEMARY AND HONEY FROZEN YOGURT

For an unusual mix of flavors that work surprisingly well together, try this Italian inspired rosemary and honey recipe that mixes sweet and herbal flavors to great effect.

Makes: 8 Serves
Prep: 30 minutes plus 30 minutes chilling time and 4 hours freezing time

Ingredients:
1 ¼ Cups Greek Yogurt
1 ½ Cups Milk
2 Tbsps Cornstarch
1/2 Cup Heavy Cream
1/2 Cup Honey
2 Tbsps Corn Syrup
2 Sprigs Rosemary
Zest of Half a Lemon

Directions
1. Mix the cornstarch with 3 tablespoons of milk to make a paste
2. Put the remaining milk, cream, honey, rosemary, lemon zest, and corn syrup in a saucepan over a medium heat and bring to the boil then remove from the heat and leave to steep for 30 minutes
3. Pass through a sieve and discard the rosemary and lemon zest
4. Return to the heat and mix in the cornstarch and stir until thickened
5. Remove from the heat and stir in the yogurt
6. Chill the mixture in the refrigerator for 30 minutes
7. Transfer to an ice cream maker and follow the directions for frozen yogurt
8. Freeze for 4 hours before serving

CUCUMBER AND MINT FROZEN YOGURT

Like old fashioned English cucumber sandwiches but a dessert version, this frozen yogurt recipe uses cooling cucumber and soothing mint for a unique flavor profile.

Makes: 8 Serves
Prep: 5 minutes plus 1 hour freezing time

Ingredients:
2 Cups Greek Yogurt
1 Cup Cucumber, cubed
1 ½ Tbsps Sugar
Juice and Zest of 1 Lemon
Handful of Fresh Mint Leaves

Directions
1. Place all the ingredients in a food processor and blitz until smooth
2. Transfer to a freezer and freeze for at least an hour before serving

DULCE DE LECHE FROZEN YOGURT

If you are looking for a decadent treat that will fool your guests at a party, then look no further than this recipe which tastes exactly like a custard-based ice cream.

Makes: 8 Serves
Prep: 5 minutes plus 4 hours freezing time

Ingredients:
2 Cups Greek Yogurt
1 Cup Dulce de Leche
1 Cup Heavy Cream
1/2 Tsp Vanilla Extract
1/8 Tsp Salt

Directions
1. Place all the ingredients in a food processor and blitz until smooth
2. Transfer to an ice cream maker and process according to the instructions for frozen yogurt
3. Freeze for 4 hours before serving

NECTARINE FROZEN YOGURT

This recipe doesn't use any sugar, instead harnessing the natural sweetness of the nectarines to make a tart and delicious frozen treat for a summer's day.

Makes: 8 Serves
Prep: 10 minutes plus 4 hours freezing time

Ingredients:
2 Cups Greek Yogurt
1 Cup Nectarines
1/4 Cup Milk
Squeeze of Lemon Juice

Directions
1. Place the nectarines and milk in a blender and blitz until smooth
2. Strain through a fine mesh sieve
3. In a bowl mix the yogurt and the fruit puree
4. Transfer to an ice cream maker and follow the directions for frozen yogurt
5. Freeze for 4 hours before serving

CASHEW VEGAN FROZEN YOGURT

This recipe is perfect for vegans as it uses no dairy products and instead achieves a creamy base thanks to cashew nuts.

Makes: 6 Serves
Prep: 5 minutes plus 24 hours fermenting time and 4 hours freezing time

Ingredients:
1 ½ Cups Cashews, soaked
1 ¼ Cup Water
2 Tbsps Maple Syrup
1 Tbsp Vanilla Extract
1/4 Tbsp Probiotic Powder

Directions
1. Place all the ingredients in a food processor and blitz until completely smooth with no visible lumps
2. Transfer to a bowl, cover, and place in a warm and dry place for 24 hours until fermented
3. Transfer to an ice cream maker and follow the directions for frozen yogurt
4. Freeze for 4 hours before serving

HONEY AND CILANTRO FROZEN YOGURT

Cilantro might not be everyone's first pick for a frozen yogurt recipe but it's actually delicious and the spicy herbal notes blend beautifully with the honey and yogurt.

Makes: 8 Serves
Prep: 5 minutes plus 3 hours freezing time

Ingredients:
2 Cups Greek Yogurt
3 Tbsps Honey
1 Tbsp Vanilla Extract
Handful of Cilantro, chopped

Directions
1. Put the yogurt in the freezer for 3 hours, taking it out and whisking vigorously every 30 minutes
2. In a saucepan over a medium heat combine the cilantro, vanilla and honey and heat for 5 minutes
3. After 3 hours of freezing and whipping remove the frozen yogurt from the freezer and serve drizzled with the cilantro honey mixture

APRICOT FROZEN YOGURT

A delicious and tart frozen yogurt that works just as well with fresh apricots in summer as it does with stewed apricots in winter.

Makes: 8 Serves
Prep: 5 minutes plus 24 hours fermenting time and 4 hours freezing time

Ingredients:
2 Cups Greek Yogurt
1 Cup Apricots
1/4 Cup Milk

Directions
1. Place all the ingredients in a food processor and blitz until completely
2. Transfer to an ice cream maker and follow the directions for frozen yogurt
3. Freeze for 4 hours before serving

About The Author

JUSTIN RAMSEY

Growing up in the food industry, Justin's family operated a range of traditional and western inspired restaurants. His passion for hearty and wholesome meals enabled him to build his own catering business.

He lives in Portland, Oregon with his wife and twin girls. Justin loves educating and inspiring other families to cook and move away from processed ingredients.

Stay connected to Justin's future publications at
www.bookwormhaven.com

One Last Thing...

If you enjoyed this book or found it useful I'd be very grateful if you'd post a short review on Amazon.

Your support really does make a difference and I read all the reviews personally so I can get your feedback and make this book even better.

Thanks again for your support!

Justin

22504949R00068

Printed in Great Britain
by Amazon